# Traditional Scottish Favour[ites]

## for Keyboard

CW00422120

| | |
|---|---|
| Afton Water | 2 |
| Annie Laurie | 4 |
| Auld Lang Syne | 6 |
| The Blue Bell Of Scotland | 8 |
| Bonnie Dundee | 10 |
| Bring Back My Bonnie To Me | 12 |
| Charlie Is My Darling | 14 |
| Green Grow The Rashes O' | 16 |
| The Gypsy Rover | 18 |
| The Hundred Pipers | 20 |
| I Belong To Glasgow | 22 |
| I Love A Lassie | 24 |
| The Keel Row | 26 |
| Loch Lomond | 28 |
| My Love, She's But A Lassie Yet | 30 |
| On The Banks Of Allan Water | 32 |
| Roamin' In The Gloamin' | 34 |
| Scotland The Brave | 36 |
| Scots, Wha Hae Wi' Wallace Bled | 38 |
| Skye Boat Song | 40 |
| The Tartan | 42 |
| Will Ye No Come Back Again? | 44 |
| Ye Banks And Braes | 46 |

Music arranged and processed by Barnes Music Engraving Ltd
East Sussex TN22 4HA, UK

Cover design by xheight design limited

**Published 1996**

**International MUSIC Publications**

International Music Publications Limited
Griffin House 161 Hammersmith Road London W6 8BS England

# Afton Water

Words by Robert Burns / Music traditional

**Suggested Registration:** Flute
**Rhythm:** Waltz
**Tempo:** ♩ = 88

1    Flow gently, sweet Afton, amang thy green braes,
      Flow gently, I'll sing thee a song in thy praise.
      My Mary's asleep by thy murmuring stream.
      Flow gently, sweet Afton, disturb not her dream.

2    Thou stock-dove, whose echo resounds thro' the glen,
      Ye wild whistling blackbirds in yon thorny den,
      Thou green-crested lapwing, thy screaming forbear,
      I charge you, disturb not my slumbering fair.

3    How lofty, sweet Afton, thy neighbouring hills,
      Far marked with the courses of clear winding rills.
      There, daily I wander as morn rises high,
      My flocks and my Mary's sweet cot in my eye.

4    How pleasant thy banks and green valleys below,
      Where wild in the woodlands the primroses blow!
      There oft as mild evening creeps over the lea,
      The sweet-scented birk shades my Mary and me.

5    The crystal stream, Afton, how lovely it glides,
      And winds by the cot where my Mary resides!
      How wanton thy waters her snowy feet lave,
      As gathering sweet flow'rets she stems thy clear wave!

6    Flow gently, sweet Afton, amang thy green braes,
      Flow gently, sweet river, the theme of my lays.
      My Mary's asleep by thy murmuring stream.
      Flow gently, sweet Afton, disturb not her dream.

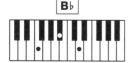
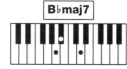
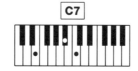
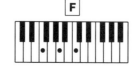
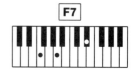

# Annie Laurie

Words by Lady John Scott / Music traditional

**Suggested Registration:** Piano
**Rhythm:** Soft Rock
**Tempo:** ♩ = 92

Max - wel - ton braes are bon - nie, where ear - ly fa's the dew, and it's there that An - nie Laur - ie gie'd me her prom - ise true, gie'd me her prom - ise true, which ne'er for - got will be, and for bon - nie An - nie___ Laur - ie, I'd___ lay_____ me doon and dee.

1   Maxwelton braes are bonnie,
     Where early fa's the dew,
     And it's there that Annie Laurie
     Gie'd me her promise true,
     Gie'd me her promise true,
     Which ne'er forgot will be,
     And for bonnie Annie Laurie,
     I'd lay me doon and dee.

2   Her brow is like the snaw-drift,
     Her neck is like the swan.
     Her face, it is the fairest
     That e'er the sun shone on,
     That e'er the sun shone on,
     And dark blue is her e'e,
     And for bonnie Annie Laurie,
     I'd lay me doon and dee.

3   Like dew on the gowan lying,
     Is the fa' o' her fairy feet,
     And like winds in summer sighing,
     Her voice is low and sweet,
     Her voice is low and sweet,
     And she's a' the world to me,
     And for bonnie Annie Laurie,
     I'd lay me doon and dee.

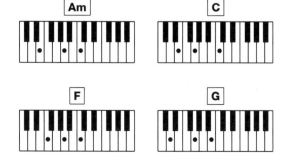

# Auld Lang Syne

Words by Robert Burns / Music traditional

**Suggested Registration:** Accordian
**Rhythm:** Soft Rock
**Tempo:** ♩ = 96

Should auld ac-quaint - ance be for - got, and

ne - ver brought to mind? Should auld ac - quaint - ance

be for - got, and days o' lang_____

syne. *For auld_____ lang_____ syne, my dear, for*

*auld_____ lang_____ syne, we'll tak' a cup o'*

*kind - ness yet, for___ auld_____ lang_____ syne.*

1 Should auld acquaintance be forgot,
And never brought to mind?
Should auld acquaintance be forgot,
And days o' lang syne.
 *For auld lang syne, my dear,*
 *For auld lang syne,*
 *We'll tak' a cup o' kindness yet,*
 *For auld lang syne.*

2 We twa hae run about the braes,
And pu'd the gowans fine,
But we've wander'd mony a weary foot,
Sin' auld lang syne.
 *For auld lang syne . . .*

3 We twa hae paidl't in the burn,
Frae morning sun till dine,
But seas between us braid hae roared
Sin' auld lang syne.
 *For auld lang syne . . .*

4 And there's a hand my trusty frien',
And gie's a hand o' thine,
And we'll tak' a right gude willy-waught,
For auld lang syne.
 *For auld lang syne . . .*

5 And surely ye'll be your pint stoup,
And surely I'll be mine!
And we'll tak' a cup o' kindness yet,
For auld lang syne.
 *For auld lang syne . . .*

**Bb**
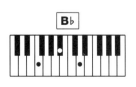

**C7**
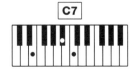

**Dm**
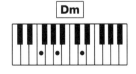

**F**
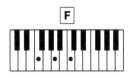

**F7**

**Gm7**

# THE BLUE BELL OF SCOTLAND

Words by Mrs Grant / Music traditional

**Suggested Registration:** Piccolo
**Rhythm:** March / Soft Rock
**Tempo:** ♩ = 116

1   Oh where, tell me, where is your highland laddie gone?
    Oh where, tell me, where is your highland laddie gone?
    He's gone with streaming banners, where noble deeds are done,
    And it's oh, in my heart, how I wish him safe at home.

2   Oh where, tell me, where did your highland laddie dwell?
    Oh where, tell me, where did your highland laddie dwell?
    He dwelt in bonnie Scotland, where blooms the sweet blue bell,
    And it's oh, in my heart, how I love my laddie well.

3   Oh what, tell me, what if your highland lad be slain?
    Oh what, tell me, what if your highland lad be slain?
    Oh no, true love will be his guard, and bring him safe again,
    For it's oh, my heart would break, if my highland lad were slain.

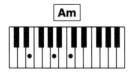
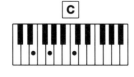
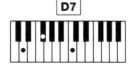
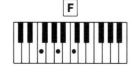
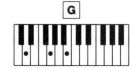

# Bonnie Dundee

By Sir Walter Scott

**Suggested Registration:** Bagpipes
**Rhythm:** Slow Rock 6/8
**Tempo:** ♩. = 63

To the Lords of con-ven-tion 'twas Cla-ver-house spoke, 'Ere the

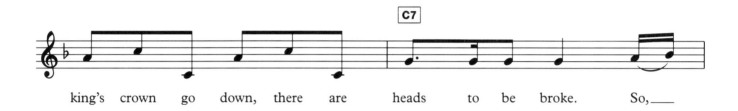

king's crown go down, there are heads to be broke. So,___

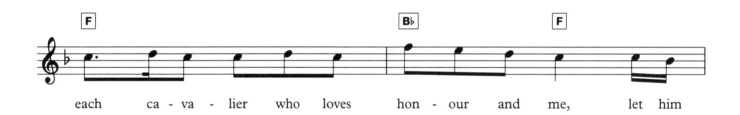

each ca-va-lier who loves hon-our and me, let him

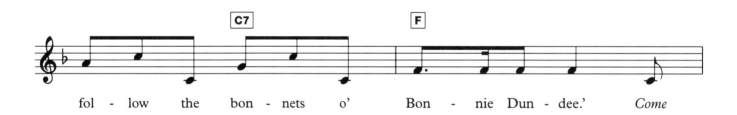

fol-low the bon-nets o' Bon - nie Dun-dee.' *Come*

*fill up my cup,___ come fill up my can, come*

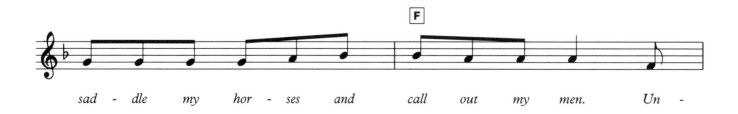

*sad-dle my hor-ses and call out my men.* Un-

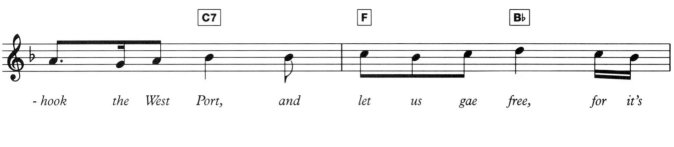

- hook     the     West     Port,     and     let     us     gae     free,     for     it's

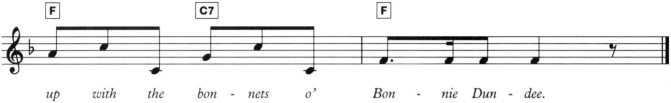

up     with     the     bon - nets     o'     Bon - nie Dun - dee.

1     To the Lords of convention 'twas Claverhouse spoke,
       'Ere the king's crown go down, there are heads to be broke.
       So, each cavalier who loves honour and me,
       Let him follow the bonnets o' Bonnie Dundee.'
          *Come fill up my cup, come fill up my can,*
          *Come saddle my horses and call out my men.*
          *Unhook the West Port, and let us gae free,*
          *For it's up with the bonnets o' Bonnie Dundee.*

2     Dundee, he is mounted, he rides up the street.
       The bells they ring backward, the drums they are beat,
       But the provost (douce man) said 'Just e'en let it be,
       For the toun is weel rid o' that de'il o' Dundee.'
          *Come fill up my cup, come . . .*

3     There are hills beyond Pentland, and lands beyond Forth.
       Be there lords in the south, there are chiefs in the north.
       There are brave Duinnewassels, three thousand times three
       Will cry, 'Hey for the bonnets o' Bonnie Dundee.'
          *Come fill up my cup, come . . .*

4     Then awa' to the hills, to the lea, to the rocks.
       Ere I own a usurper, I'll couch with the fox,
       And tremble, false whigs, in the midst o' your glee.
       Ye hae no seen the last o' my bonnets and me.
          *Come fill up my cup, come . . .*

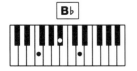 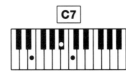 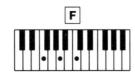

# Bring Back My Bonnie To Me

Traditional

**Suggested Registration:** Piano
**Rhythm:** Waltz
**Tempo:** ♩ = 152

My Bon - nie lies o - ver the

o - cean,_____ my Bon - nie lies

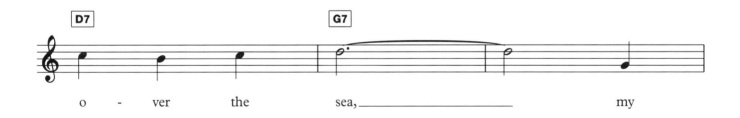

o - ver the sea,_____ my

Bon - nie lies o - ver the o - cean,_____

oh, bring back my Bon - nie to me.

Bring back, oh bring

back, oh bring back my Bon - nie to me, to

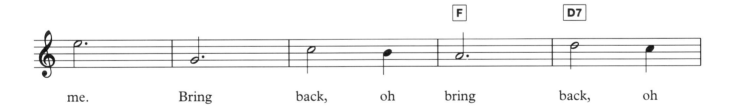

me. Bring back, oh bring back, oh

bring back my Bon - nie to me.

# CHARLIE IS MY DARLING

Words by Robert Burns / Music traditional

**Suggested Registration:** Violin
**Rhythm:** Shuffle
**Tempo:** ♩. = 108

Char - lie is my dar - ling, my dar - ling, my dar - ling.

Char - lie is my dar - ling, the young____ che - va -

- lier. As he was walk - ing up the street, the

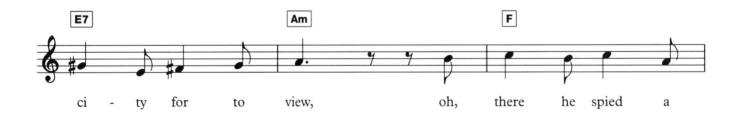

ci - ty for to view, oh, there he spied a

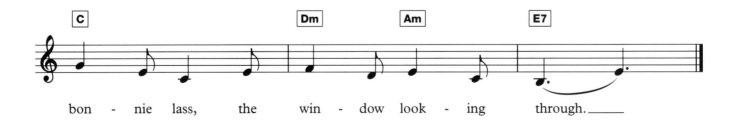

bon - nie lass, the win - dow look - ing through.____

*Charlie is my darling,*
*My darling, my darling.*
*Charlie is my darling,*
*The young chevalier.*

1   As he was walking up the street,
The city for to view,
Oh, there he spied a bonnie lass,
The window looking through.
  *Charlie is my darling . . .*

2   Sae light's he jumped up the stair,
And tirled at the pin,
And wha sae ready as hersel'
To let the laddie in.
  *Charlie is my darling . . .*

3   He set his Jenny on his knee,
All in his highland dress,
For brawly weel he kend the way
To please a bonnie lass.
  *Charlie is my darling . . .*

4   It's up yon heathery mountain,
And down yon scraggy glen,
We daurna gang a-milking,
For Charlie and his men.
  *Charlie is my darling . . .*

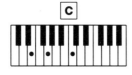
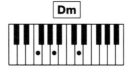
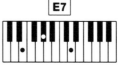
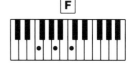

# GREEN GROW THE RASHES O'

Words by Robert Burns / Music traditional

**Suggested Registration:** French Horn
**Rhythm:** March
**Tempo:** ♩ = 96

There's nocht but care on ev-ery han', in ev-ery hour that pass-es, O', what

sig - ni-fies the life o' man, an' twer - na for the lass - es, O'.

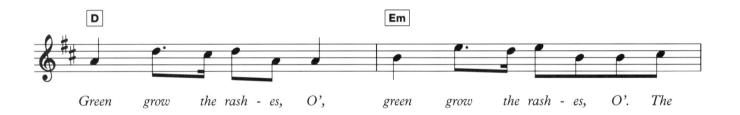

*Green grow the rash - es, O', green grow the rash - es, O'. The*

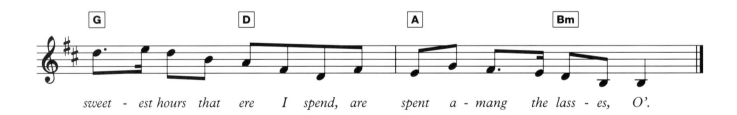

*sweet - est hours that ere I spend, are spent a - mang the lass - es, O'.*

1   There's nocht but care on every han',
    In every hour that passes, O',
    What signifies the life o' man,
    An' twerna for the lasses, O'.
      *Green grow the rashes, O',*
      *Green grow the rashes, O'.*
      *The sweetest hours that ere I spend,*
      *Are spent amang the lasses, O'.*

2   The warldly race may riches chase,
    And riches still may fly them, O',
    An' tho' at last they catch them fast,
    Their hearts can ne'er enjoy them, O'.
      *Green grow . . .*

3   Gie me a canny hour at e'en,
    My arm aboot my dearie, O',
    An' war'ly cares an' war'ly men,
    May a' gae tapsalteerie, O'.
      *Green grow . . .*

4   For ye sae douce, wha sneer at this,
    Ye're nocht but senseless asses, O'.
    The wisest man the warl' e'er saw,
    He dearly lo'ed the lasses, O'.
      *Green grow . . .*

5   Auld nature swears, the lovely dears,
    Her noblest work she classes, O'.
    Her 'prentice han' she tried on man,
    An' then she made the lasses, O'.
      *Green grow . . .*

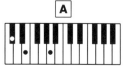
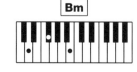
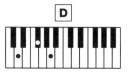
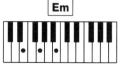
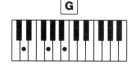

# THE GYPSY ROVER

Traditional

**Suggested Registration:** Flute
**Rhythm:** Soft Rock
**Tempo:** ♩ = 108

1   The gypsy rover came over the hill,
    Bound through the valley so shady.
    He whistled, and he sang till the green woods rang,
    And he won the heart of a lady.
        *Ah di do, ah di do da day,*
        *Ah di do, ah di day dee.*
        *He whistled and he sang*
        *Till the green woods rang,*
        *And he won the heart of a lady.*

2   She left her father's castle gate,
    She left her own true lover.
    She left her servants and her estate,
    To follow the gypsy rover.
        *Ah di do . . .*

3   Her father saddled his fastest steed,
    Roamed the valley all over,
    Sought his daughter at great speed,
    And the whistling gypsy rover.
        *Ah di do . . .*

4   He came at last to a mansion fine,
    Down by the river Claydie,
    And there was music, and there was wine,
    For the gypsy and his lady.
        *Ah di do . . .*

5   'He's no gypsy, my father' said she,
    'My lord of freelands all over,
    And I will stay till my dying day,
    With my whistling gypsy rover.'
        *Ah di do . . .*

C
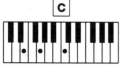

D7
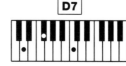

G
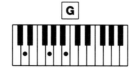

# The Hundred Pipers

Words by Lady Nairne / Music traditional

**Suggested Registration:** Bagpipes
**Rhythm:** Slow Rock 6/8
**Tempo:** ♩. = 76

Wi' a hun-dred pi-pers an' a', an' a', wi' a hun-dred pi-pers an'

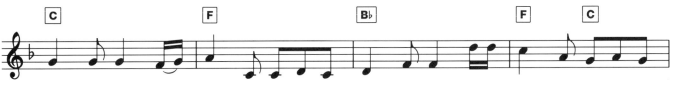

a', an' a', we'll up an' gie 'em a blaw, a blaw, wi' a hun-dred pi-pers an'

a', an' a'. Oh, it's ower the bor-der a - wa', a-wa', it's_ ower the bor-der a -

- wa', a-wa', we'll on an' we'll march to Car-lisle ha', wi' its Yetts, its Cas-tell an'

a, an' a. *Wi' a hun-dred pi-pers an' a', an' a', wi' a hun-dred pi-pers an'*

*a', an' a', we'll up and gie 'em a blaw, a blaw, wi' a hun-dred pi-pers an' a', an' a'.*

1    Wi' a hundred pipers an' a', an' a',
Wi' a hundred pipers an' a', an' a',
We'll up an' gie 'em a blaw, a blaw,
Wi' a hundred pipers an' a', an' a'.
Oh, it's ower the border awa', awa',
It's ower the border awa', awa',
We'll on an' we'll march to Carlisle ha',
Wi' its Yetts, its Castell an' a, an' a.
*Wi' a hundred pipers an' a', an' a',*
*Wi' a hundred pipers an' a', an' a',*
*We'll up and gie 'em a blaw, a blaw,*
*Wi' a hundred pipers an' a', an' a'.*

2    Oh! Our sodger lads look'd braw, look'd braw,
Wi' their tartans, kilts, an' a', an' a',
Wi' their bonnets, an' feathers, an' glitt'ring gear,
An' pibrochs sounding sweet an' clear.
Will they a' return to their ain dear glen?
Will they a' return – our Hieland men?
Second-sighted Sandy looked fu' wae,
And mothers grat when they march'd awa'.
*Wi' a hundred pipers an' a', an' a',*
*Wi' a hundred pipers an' a', an' a',*
*But they'll up an' gie 'em a blaw, a blaw,*
*Wi' a hundred pipers an' a', an' a'.*

3    Oh! Wha is foremaist o' a', o' a'?
Oh! Wha does follow the blaw, the blaw?
Bonnie Charlie, the king o' us a', hurra!
Wi' his hundred pipers an' a', an' a'!
His bonnet an' feathers he's waving high!
His prancing steed maist seems to fly!
The nor' wind plays with his curly hair,
While the pipers blaw in an unco flare!
*Wi' a hundred pipers an' a', an' a',*
*Wi' a hundred pipers an' a', an' a',*
*We'll up an' gie 'em a blaw, a blaw,*
*Wi' a hundred pipers an' a', an' a'.*

4    The Esk was swollen, sae red, sae deep,
But shouther to shouther the brave lads keep,
Twa thousand swam ower to fell English ground,
An' danc'd themselves dry to the pibroch's sound.
Dumfoundered, the English saw, they saw!
Dumfoundered they heard the blaw, the blaw!
Dumfoundered, they a' ran awa', awa',
Frae the hundred pipers an' a', an' a'!
*Wi' a hundred pipers an' a', an' a',*
*Wi' a hundred pipers an' a', an' a',*
*We'll up an' gie 'em a blaw, a blaw,*
*Wi' a hundred pipers an' a', an' a'.*

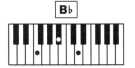
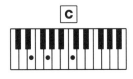
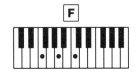

# I Belong To Glasgow

Words and Music by Will Fyffe

**Suggested Registration:** Accordian
**Rhythm:** Waltz
**Tempo:** ♩ = 160

I    be - long    to    Glas - gow,_____

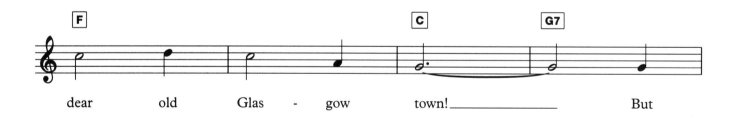

dear    old    Glas - gow    town!_____    But

what's    the    mat - ter    with    Glas - gow,    for    it's

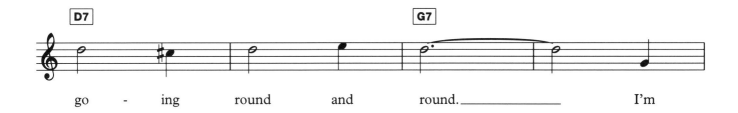

go - ing round and round._____ I'm

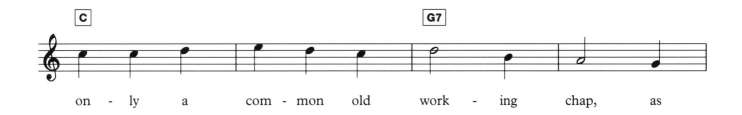

on - ly a com - mon old work - ing chap, as

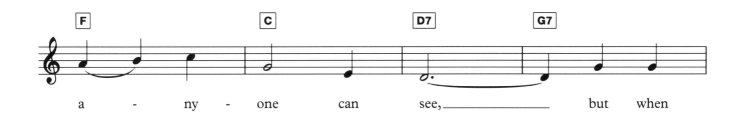

a - ny - one can see,_____ but when

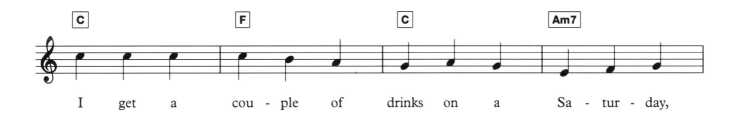

I get a cou - ple of drinks on a Sa - tur - day,

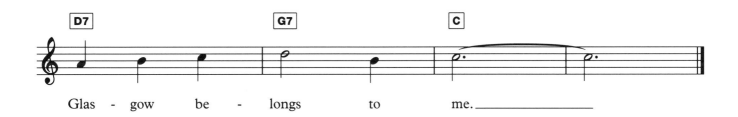

Glas - gow be - longs to me._____

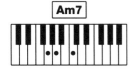
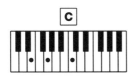
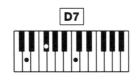
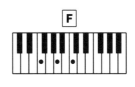

# I Love A Lassie

Words and Music by Harry Lauder and Gerald Grafton

**Suggested Registration:** Clarinet
**Rhythm:** March
**Tempo:** ♩ = 112

I love a lass - ie, a bon - nie Hie - lan' lass - ie, if ye

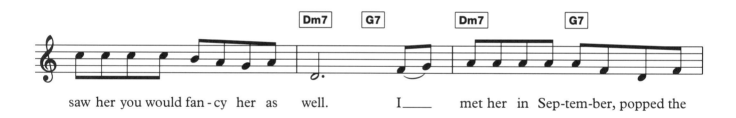

saw her you would fan - cy her as well. I___ met her in Sep - tem - ber, popped the

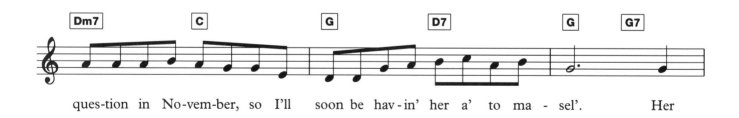

ques - tion in No - vem - ber, so I'll soon be hav - in' her a' to ma - sel'. Her

fai - ther has con - sent - ed, so I'm feel - ing quite con - tent - ed, 'cause I've

# THE KEEL ROW

Traditional

**Suggested Registration:** Piccolo
**Rhythm:** Shuffle
**Tempo:** ♩ = 112

Oh, who is like my John - nie, sae leish, sae blyth, sae bon - nie! He's

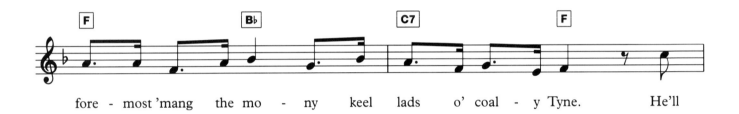

fore - most 'mang the mo - ny keel lads o' coal - y Tyne. He'll

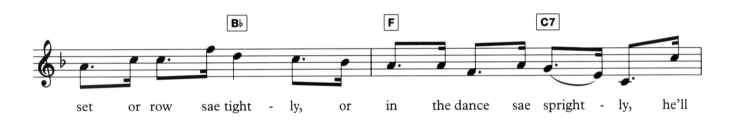

set or row sae tight - ly, or in the dance sae spright - ly, he'll

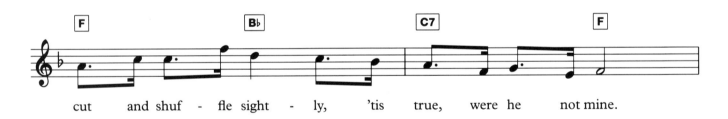

cut and shuf - fle sight - ly, 'tis true, were he not mine.

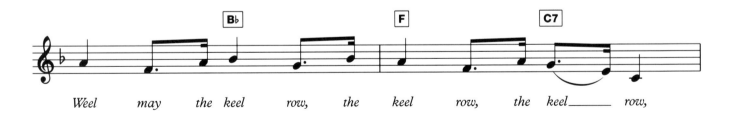

*Weel may the keel row, the keel row, the keel____ row,*

*weel may the keel row that my____ lad's____ in.*

1   Oh, who is like my Johnnie,
    Sae leish, sae blyth, sae bonnie!
    He's foremost 'mang the mony
    Keel lads o' coaly Tyne.
    He'll set or row sae tightly,
    Or in the dance sae sprightly,
    He'll cut and shuffle sightly,
    'Tis true, were he not mine.
        *Weel may the keel row,*
        *The keel row, the keel row,*
        *Weel may the keel row that my lad's in.*

2   He has na mair o' learning,
    Than tells his weekly earning.
    Yet right frae wrang discerning,
    Though brave, nae bruiser he.
    Though he no worth a plack is,
    His ain coat on his back is,
    And nane can say that black is
    The white of Johnnie's e'e.
        *Weel may the keel row . . .*

3   He wears a blue bonnet,
    Blue bonnet, blue bonnet,
    He wears a blue bonnet,
    A dimple's in his chin,
    And weel may the keel row,
    The keel row, the keel row,
    And weel may the keel row,
    That my lad's in.
        *Weel may the keel row . . .*

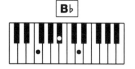

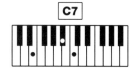

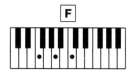

# Loch Lomond

Traditional

**Suggested Registration:** Accordian
**Rhythm:** Soft Rock
**Tempo:** ♩ = 96

By yon bon-nie banks and by yon bon-nie braes, where the

suns shines bright on Loch Lo - mond, where I and my true love were

ev - er wont to gae, on the bon-nie bon-nie banks of Loch Lo - mond. *Oh!*

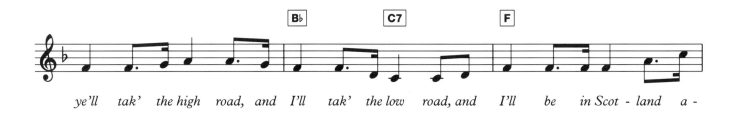

*ye'll tak' the high road, and I'll tak' the low road, and I'll be in Scot - land a -*

*- fore ye, but I and my true love will ne - ver meet a - gain, on the*

*bon - nie bon - nie banks of Loch Lo - mond.*

1   By yon bonnie banks and by yon bonnie braes,
    Where the suns shines bright on Loch Lomond,
    Where I and my true love were ever wont to gae,
    On the bonnie bonnie banks of Loch Lomond.
        *Oh! ye'll tak' the high road,*
        *And I'll tak' the low road,*
        *And I'll be in Scotland afore ye,*
        *But I and my true love will never meet again,*
        *On the bonnie bonnie banks of Loch Lomond.*

2   'Twas there that we parted in yon shady glen,
    On the steep, steep side o' Ben Lomond,
    Where in purple hue the Hieland hills we view,
    An' the moon comin' out in the gloaming.
        *Oh! ye'll tak' the . . .*

3   The wee birdies sing, and the wild flowers spring,
    An' in sunshine the waters are sleeping,
    But the broken heart, it kens nae second spring,
    Tho' the waeful may cease frae their greeting.
        *Oh! ye'll tak' the . . .*

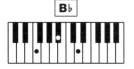 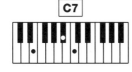 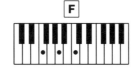

# My Love, She's But A Lassie Yet

Traditional

**Suggested Registration:** Piano
**Rhythm:** Country Rock
**Tempo:** ♩ = 144

My__ love, she's but a lass - ie yet, my__

love, she's but a lass - ie yet! We'll__ let her stand a

year or twa, she'll no__ be__ half sae sau - cy yet! I____

rue the day I sought her. Oh! I____ rue the day I

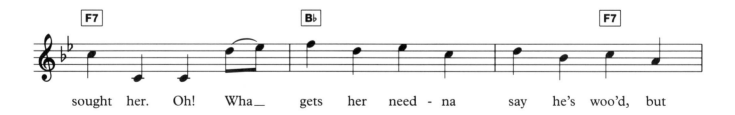

sought her. Oh! Wha__ gets her need - na say he's woo'd, but

he__ may__ say he's bought her. Oh!

*My love, she's but a lassie yet,*
*My love, she's but a lassie yet!*
*We'll let her stand a year or twa,*
*She'll no be half sae saucy yet!*

1   Oh! I rue the day I sought her.
    Oh! I rue the day I sought her.
    Oh! Wha gets her needna say he's woo'd,
    But he may say he's bought her, oh!
    *My love, she's but . . .*

2   Come draw a drap o' the best o't yet,
    Come draw a drap o' the best o't yet!
    Gae seek for pleasure where ye will,
    But here I never missed it yet.
    *My love, she's but . . .*

3   We're a' dry wi' drinkin' o't,
    We're a' dry wi' drinkin' o't!
    The minister kiss't the fiddler's wife,
    He couldna preach for thinkin' o't!
    *My love, she's but . . .*

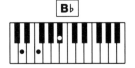
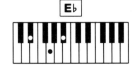
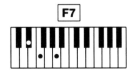

# On The Banks Of Allan Water

Traditional

**Suggested Registration:** Flute
**Rhythm:** Waltz
**Tempo:** ♩ = 84

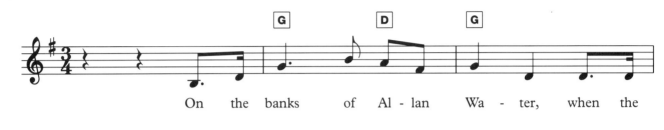

On the banks of Al - lan Wa - ter, when the

sweet spring-time did fall,_____ was the mill - er's love - ly

daugh - ter, fair - est of them all. For the

bride, a sol - dier sought her, and a win - ning tongue had

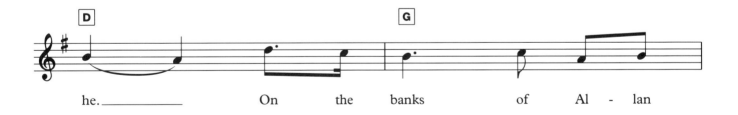

he._____ On the banks of Al - lan

Wa - ter, none so gay as she.

1 On the banks of Allan Water,
  When the sweet springtime did fall,
  Was the miller's lovely daughter,
  Fairest of them all.
  For the bride, a soldier sought her,
  And a winning tongue had he.
  On the banks of Allan Water,
  None so gay as she.

2 On the banks of Allan Water,
  When brown autumn spreads its store,
  There I saw the miller's daughter,
  But she smiled no more.
  For the summer grief had brought her,
  And the soldier false was he.
  On the banks of Allan Water,
  None so sad as she.

3 On the banks of Allan Water,
  When the winter snow fell fast,
  Still was seen the miller's daughter.
  Chilling blew the blast,
  But the miller's lovely daughter,
  Both from cold and care was free.
  On the banks of Allan Water,
  There a corpse lay she.

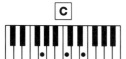
C

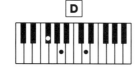
D

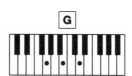
G

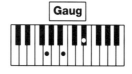
Gaug

# Roamin' In The Gloamin'

Words and Music by Harry Lauder

**Suggested Registration:** Piano
**Rhythm:** Soft Rock
**Tempo:** ♩ = 138

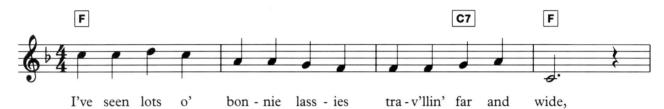

I've seen lots o' bon - nie lass - ies tra - v'llin' far and wide,

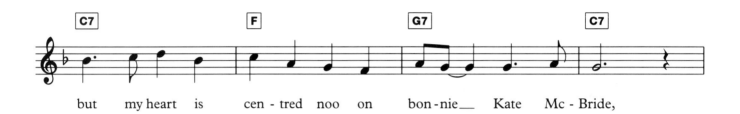

but my heart is cen - tred noo on bon - nie__ Kate Mc - Bride,

and al - tho' I'm no' a chap that throws a word a - way,

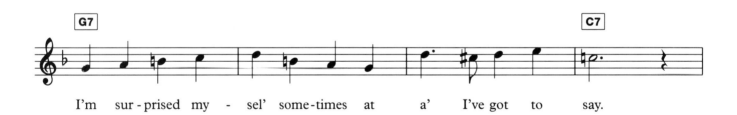

I'm sur - prised my - sel' some - times at a' I've got to say.

*Roam - in' in the gloam - in', on the bon - nie__ banks o' Clyde,*

*roam - in' in the gloam - in' wae my lass - ie by my side.* When the

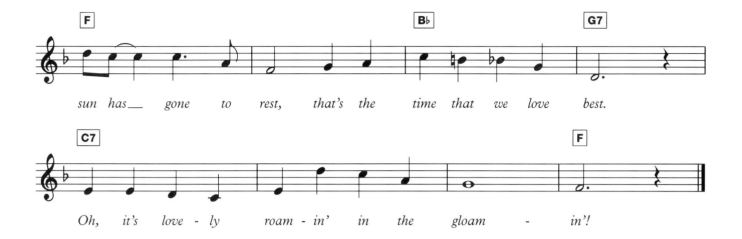

sun has___ gone to rest, that's the time that we love best.

Oh, it's love - ly roam - in' in the gloam - in'!

1  I've seen lots o' bonnie lassies trav'llin' far and wide,
   But my heart is centred noo on bonnie Kate McBride,
   And altho' I'm no' a chap that throws a word away,
   I'm surprised mysel' sometimes at a' I've got to say.
       *Roamin' in the gloamin', on the bonnie banks o' Clyde,*
       *Roamin' in the gloamin' wae my lassie by my side.*
       *When the sun has gone to rest, that's the time that we love best.*
       *Oh, it's lovely roamin' in the gloamin'!*

2  One nicht in the gloamin' we were trippin' side by side.
   I kissed her twice, and asked her once if she would be my bride.
   She was shy, so was I, we were baith the same,
   But I got brave and braver on the journey comin' hame.
       *Roamin' in the gloamin'. . .*

3  Last nicht efter strollin' we got hame at half-past nine.
   Sittin' at the kitchen fire, I asked her to be mine.
   When she promised, I got up and danced the Hielan' fling.
   I've just been at the jew'ller's, and I've picked a nice wee ring.
       *Roamin' in the gloamin'. . .*

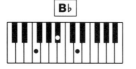 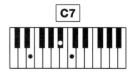 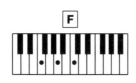 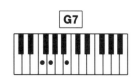

# Scotland The Brave

Traditional

**Suggested Registration:** Bagpipes
**Rhythm:** March
**Tempo:** ♩ = 100

Hark when the night is fall - ing, hear, hear the pipes are call - ing,

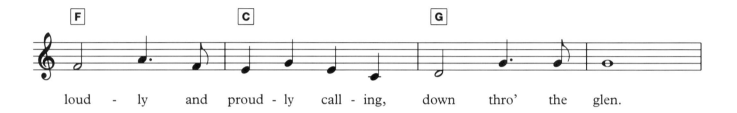

loud - ly and proud - ly call - ing, down thro' the glen.

There where the hills are sleep - ing, now feel the blood a - leap - ing,

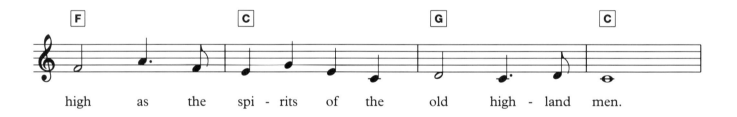

high as the spi - rits of the old high - land men.

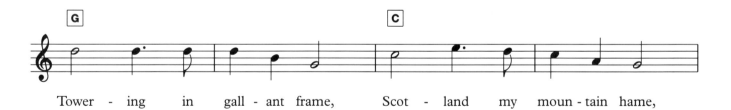

Tower - ing in gall - ant frame, Scot - land my moun - tain hame,

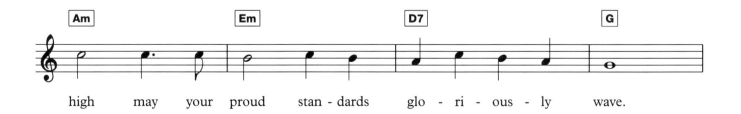

high may your proud stan - dards glo - ri - ous - ly wave.

Land of my high en-dea-vour, land of the shin-ing sil-ver,

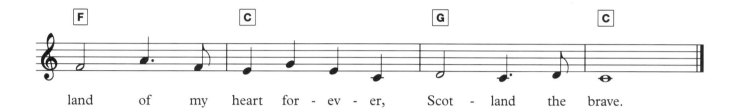

land of my heart for-ev-er, Scot-land the brave.

1  Hark when the night is falling,
   Hear, hear the pipes are calling,
   Loudly and proudly calling,
   Down thro' the glen.
   There where the hills are sleeping,
   Now feel the blood a-leaping,
   High as the spirits of the
   Old highland men.
   Towering in gallant frame,
   Scotland my mountain hame,
   High may your proud standards
   Gloriously wave.
   Land of my high endeavour,
   Land of the shining silver,
   Land of my heart forever,
   Scotland the brave.

2  High in the misty highlands
   Out by the purple islands,
   Brave are the hearts that beat
   Beneath Scottish skies.
   Wild are the winds to meet you,
   Staunch are the friends that greet you,
   Kind as the love that shines from
   Fair maidens' eyes.
   Towering in gallant frame,
   Scotland my mountain hame,
   High may your proud standards
   Gloriously wave.
   Land of my high endeavour,
   Land of the shining silver,
   Land of my heart forever,
   Scotland the brave.

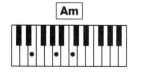
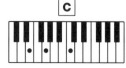

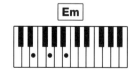
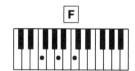

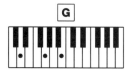

# Scots, Wha Hae Wi' Wallace Bled

Words by Robert Burns / Music traditional

**Suggested Registration:** Bagpipes
**Rhythm:** 6/8 March
**Tempo:** ♩. = 92

Scots, wha hae wi' Wal - lace bled! Scots, wham Bruce has

of - ten led!_____ Wel - come to your go - ry bed,

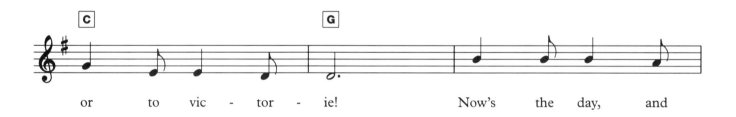

or to vic - tor - ie! Now's the day, and

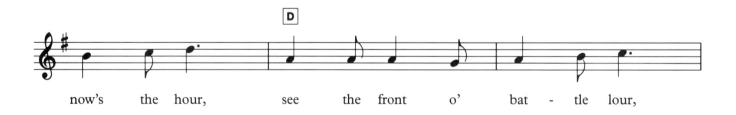

now's the hour, see the front o' bat - tle lour,

see ap-proach proud Ed - ward's pow'r, chains and sla - ver - ie!

1   Scots, wha hae wi' Wallace bled!
    Scots, wham Bruce has often led!
    Welcome to your gory bed,
    Or to victorie!
    Now's the day, and now's the hour,
    See the front o' battle lour,
    See approach proud Edward's pow'r,
    Chains and slaverie!

2   Wha would be a traitor knave?
    Wha would fill a coward's grave?
    Wha sae base as be a slave?
    Let him turn an' flee!
    Wha for Scotland's king and law,
    Freedom's sword will strongly draw,
    Freeman stand or freeman fa,
    Let him follow me!

3   By oppression's woes an' pains,
    By your sons in servile chains,
    We will drain our dearest veins,
    But we will be free!
    Lay the proud usurpers low!
    Tyrants fall in ev' ry foe!
    Liberty's in ev' ry blow,
    Let us do or dee!

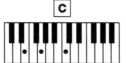
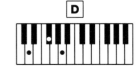
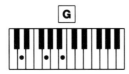

# Skye Boat Song

Words by Sir Harold Boulton / Music by Annie McLeod

**Suggested Registration:** Flute
**Rhythm:** Slow Rock 6/8
**Tempo:** ♩. = 40

*'Speed bonnie boat, like a bird on the wing,*
*Onward,' the sailors cry,*
*'Carry the boy that's born to be king,*
*Over the sea to Skye.'*

1  Loud the winds howl, loud the waves roar,
Thunder clouds rend the air.
Baffled, our foes stand on the shore,
Follow they will not dare.
    *'Speed bonnie boat . . .*

2  Though the waves leap, soft shall ye sleep,
Ocean's a royal bed.
Rocked in the deep, Flora will keep
Watch by your weary head.
    *'Speed bonnie boat . . .*

3  Many's the lad fought on that day,
Well the claymore could wield.
When the night came, silently lay
Dead on Culloden's field.
    *'Speed bonnie boat . . .*

4  Burned are our homes, exile and death
Scatter the loyal men.
Yet, e'er the sword cool in the sheath,
Charlie will come again.
    *'Speed bonnie boat . . .*

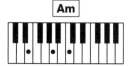
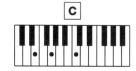
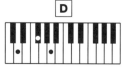
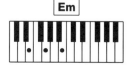

# The Tartan

Words by Sydney Bell / Music by Kenneth McKellar

**Suggested Registration:** Trumpet
**Rhythm:** March
**Tempo:** ♩ = 108

There are hun - dreds of tar - tans so love - ly to

see, and ma - ny a fa - mous has graced the bare___

knee, and the sett that I wear is both an - cient and

braw, it's the pride o' my heart, and the dear - est of

a'. Then it's hey! for the tar - tan, and ho! for the

tar - tan! The stamp o' the Hie - lands from Skye to Dun -

- dee, and it's proud I am bear - ing the tar - tan I'm

wear - ing, the pride o' my clan and the tar - tan for me!

1    There are hundreds of tartans so lovely to see,
And many a famous has graced the bare knee,
And the sett that I wear is both ancient and braw,
It's the pride o' my heart, and the dearest of a'.
*Then it's hey! for the tartan, and ho! for the tartan!*
*The stamp o' the Hielands from Skye to Dundee,*
*And it's proud I am bearing the tartan I'm wearing,*
*The pride o' my clan and the tartan for me!*

2    The Mackenzie is noted, the Lindsay is grand,
The Gordon's familiar in many a land,
And the Cameron men have a right to be proud,
With the Campbells and Stewarts, MacLeod of MacLeod.
*Then it's hey! for the tartan . . .*

3    There's the Bruce, the Buchanan, the Fraser and MacBean,
MacDonald, Macmillan, Macpherson and MacLean,
But I can't name them all, and it's no use to try,
So I give you, 'The Tartan, from Solway to Skye!'
*Then it's hey! for the tartan . . .*

4    Aye! The children of Scotia may roam the world o'er,
But their thoughts aye return to the land they adore,
And the skirl o' the pipes sends the heart beating high,
And the Tartans of home bring a tear to the eye.
*Then it's hey! for the tartan . . .*

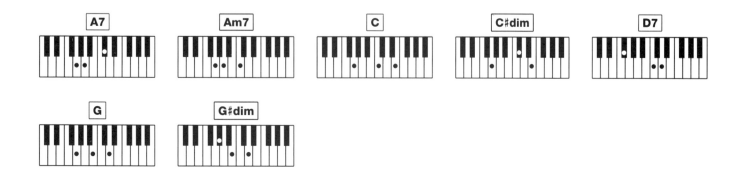

# WILL YE NO COME BACK AGAIN?

Words by Lady Nairne / Music traditional

**Suggested Registration:** Piano
**Rhythm:** Soft Rock
**Tempo:** ♩ = 104

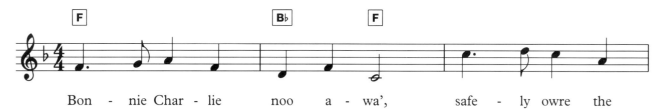

Bon - nie Char - lie noo a - wa', safe - ly owre the

friend - ly main. Mo - ny a heart will break in twa',

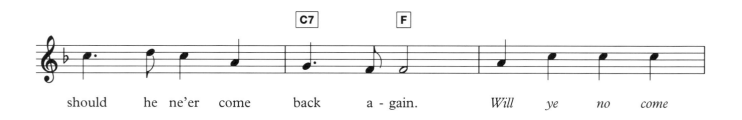

should he ne'er come back a - gain. *Will ye no come*

*back a - gain? Will ye no come back___ a - gain?*

*Bet - ter lo'ed ye can - na be. Will ye no come back a-gain?*

1 Bonnie Charlie noo awa',
Safely owre the friendly main.
Mony a heart will break in twa',
Should he ne' er come back again.
*Will ye no come back again?*
*Will ye no come back again?*
*Better lo'ed ye canna be.*
*Will ye no come back again?*

2 Ye trusted in your Hieland men,
They trusted you, dear Charlie!
They kent your hiding in the glen,
Death or exile braving.
*Will ye no come back . . .*

3 English bribes were a' in vain,
Tho' puir and puirer we maun be,
Siller canna buy the heart
That beats aye for thine and thee.
*Will ye no come back . . .*

4 We watched thee in the gloaming hour,
We watched thee in the morning grey,
Tho' thirty thousand pound they gie.
Oh, there is nane that wad betray!
*Will ye no come back . . .*

5 Sweet's the laverock's note and lang,
Lilting wildly up the glen,
But aye to me he sings ae sang,
'Will ye no come back again?'
*Will ye no come back . . .*

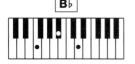
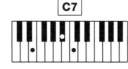
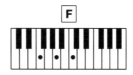

# Ye Banks And Braes

Words by Robert Burns / Music traditional

**Suggested Registration:** Flute
**Rhythm:** Slow Rock 6/8
**Tempo:** ♩. = 44

Ye banks and braes_ o' bon - nie Doon, how

can___ ye bloom_ sae fresh_ and fair? How can ye chaunt, ye

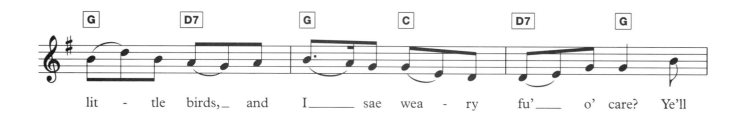

lit - tle birds,_ and I___ sae wea - ry fu'___ o' care? Ye'll

break my heart,_ ye warb - ling birds,_ that wan - ton through the

flow - 'ry thorn. Ye mind me o'___ de - part - ed joys,_ de -

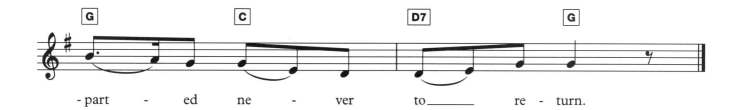

- part - ed ne - ver to———— re - turn.

1   Ye banks and braes o' bonnie Doon,
How can ye bloom sae fresh and fair?
How can ye chaunt, ye little birds,
And I sae weary fu' o' care?
Ye'll break my heart, ye warbling birds,
That wanton through the flow'ry thorn.
Ye mind me o' departed joys,
Departed never to return.

2   Oft hae I roved by bonnie Doon,
By morning and by evening shine,
To hear the birds sing o' their loves,
As fondly once I sang o' mine.
Wi' lightsome heart, I stretched my hand,
And pu'd a rose bud from the tree,
But my fause lover stole the rose,
And left, and left the thorn wi' me.

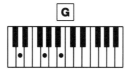

Printed and bound in Great Britain 2/01

# The Easy Keyboard Library

## also available in this series

**Country Songs**
including:
Don't It Make My Brown Eye's Blue,
Just When I Needed You Most,
The Rose and Stand By Your Man

**Classic Hits Volume 1**
including:
All Woman, From A Distance,
I'd Do Anything For Love
(But I Won't Do That) and Show Me Heaven

**Classic Hits Volume 2**
including:
Don't Go Breaking My Heart,
Heal The World,
My Baby Just Cares For Me and
What A Wonderful World

**Showtunes**
including:
Anything Goes, Forty-Second Street,
I Remember It Well and
Lullaby Of Broadway

**Number One Hits**
including:
Congratulations, Moon River,
Stand By Me and Without You

**Film Classics**
including:
I Will Always Love You, Chariots
Of Fire, Aces High and Mona Lisa

**Love Songs Volume 1**
including:
Careless Whisper,
The First Time Ever I Saw Your Face,
Saving All My Love For You
and True Love

**Love Songs Volume 2**
including:
I'll Be There, Love Me Tender,
Where Do I Begin? (Love Story) and
You've Lost That Lovin' Feelin'

**Christmas Songs**
including:
Another Rock & Roll Christmas,
Frosty The Snowman, Jingle Bells and
Mistletoe And Wine

**Soul Classics**
including:
Fever, My Girl, (Sittin' On) The Dock
Of The Bay and When A Man Loves
A Woman

**TV Themes**
including:
Birds Of A Feather, Coronation Street, Last
Of The Summer Wine and Match Of The Day

**Big Band Hits**
including:
Come Fly With Me, In The Mood,
It's Only A Paper Moon and Secret Love

# THE EASY KEYBOARD LIBRARY